Wild Nature

Gros...

an...

Elizabeth Laskey

www.heinemann.co.uk/library

Visit our website to find out more information about **Heinemann Library** books.

To order:

 Phone 44 (0) 1865 888066

 Send a fax to 44 (0) 1865 314091

 Visit the Heinemann Bookshop at www.heinemann.co.uk/library to browse our catalogue and order online.

First published in Great Britain by Heinemann Library, Halley Court, Jordan Hill, Oxford OX2 8EJ, part of Harcourt Education. Heinemann is a registered trademark of Harcourt Education Ltd.

© Harcourt Education Ltd 2005
First published in paperback in 2006
The moral right of the proprietor has been asserted.

Editorial: Barbara Katz & Kathy Peltan
Design: Kimberly Saar & David Poole
Picture Research: Bill Broyles
Production: Camilla Smith

Originated by Ambassador Litho Ltd
Printed in China by WKT Company Ltd.

ISBN 0 431 00223 9 (hardback)
09 08 07 06 05
10 9 8 7 6 5 4 3 2 1

ISBN 0 431 00238 X (paperback)
10 09 08 07 06
10 9 8 7 6 5 4 3 2 1

British Library Cataloguing in Publication Data
Laskey, Elizabeth
Wild Nature: Gross and Gory
578.4
A full catalogue record for this book is available from the British Library.

Acknowledgements

The publishers would like to thank the following for permission to reproduce photographs: p. **4** Tony Tilford/Oxford Scientific Films; p. **5t** Michael Durham/DRK Photo; p. **5b** Dr. Arthur Siegelman/Visuals Unlimited; pp. **6**, **23t** Stephen Dalton/NHPA; p. **7** Joe McDonald/Corbis; p. **8** Maslowski/Visuals Unlimited; p. **9** J & A Scott/NHPA; p. **10** David W. Breed/Oxford Scientific Films; p. **11** Wayne Lynch/DRK Photo; p. **12** Joe McDonald/DRK Photo; p. **13** Michael & Patricia Fogden/Corbis; p. **14** Morley Read/Nature Picture Library; p. **15** Norbert Wu/Norbert Wu Productions; p. **16** David Wrobel/Visuals Unlimited; p. **17t** Tom Mchugh/Photo Researchers, Inc.; p. **17b** David Kearnes/Seapics.com; p. **18** Jeff Foott/DRK Photo; p. **19** Michael

Cover photograph of a lamprey by David Kearnes/Seapics.com

Every effort has been made to contact copyright holders of any material reproduced in this book. Any omissions will be rectified in subsequent printings if notice is given to the publishers.

Disclaimer

All the Internet addresses (URLs) given in this book were valid at the time of going to press. However, due to the dynamic nature of the Internet, some addresses may have changed, or sites may have ceased to exist since publication. While the author and publishers regret any inconvenience this may cause readers, no responsibility for any such changes can be accepted by either the author or the publishers.

Contents

Some words are shown in bold, **like this.** You can find out what they mean by looking in the glossary.

Which rodent likes to hang out in sewers?

In this book you will meet a slimy fish that sucks out the insides of other fish. You will also learn about a flower that smells so awful it can make people pass out! People think these things are revolting. But being gross or gory is normal for these plants and animals. Sometimes it can even help them survive.

Meet the brown rat

The brown rat is also known as the sewer rat. It spends hours swimming through sewer pipes. Sometimes one will find its way into someone's toilet. That can give a person a very nasty surprise.

Brown rats are a type of **mammal** known as a rodent. Most rodents eat mostly nuts and seeds. Not the brown rat! It will eat anything it can get its paws on, including meat, grains, insects, soap, paper, rubbish and dead animals.

The brown rat is about 20 to 26 centimetres long, not including its creepy, scaly tail.

Did you know?

The brown rat can tread water (stay afloat) for three days.

Brown rats can squeeze through holes only 13 millimetres wide.

A super survivor

The brown rat is **native** to Asia. Long ago it got on to ships and was taken to most other parts of the world. It reached Europe in the 1500s and North America in the 1700s.

Brown rats are excellent survivors. They are not fussy about what they eat or where they live. They can live in city sewers and subways, or in cornfields in the country.

Rats and the plague

The brown rat and its cousin, the black rat, can spread plague. Plague is a disease that killed millions of people in Europe and Asia between the 1300s and the early 1900s. Plague is spread by fleas that carry plague **bacteria.** These fleas lived on rats and made them ill. When the rats died, the fleas jumped off the rats and bit people. The bacteria then made the people ill with plague.

You dirty rat!

Brown rats do not mind living near people. But people do mind living near brown rats. Brown rats live in large groups. They all use one area as a toilet. **Faeces** and **urine** pile up containing **bacteria** that can cause serious diseases.

Brown rats also do a lot of damage. They eat crops. They spread bacteria to stored food, which then has to be thrown away. They

Brown rats' teeth grow at least 10 centimetres a year. They chew on things like metal, brick and wiring to keep their teeth worn down.

chew on electrical wires, which sometimes causes fires. People spend a lot of money on rat poison and on 'rat-proofing' buildings and food-storage areas. But all this does not get rid of the rats. In the USA alone, the rat population is estimated at 150 to 175 million.

Which mammal fakes its own death?

When threatened by a **predator,** the common Virginia opossum makes one of several gross choices. As it cannot move fast, the opossum tries to disgust animals that want to eat it. The opossum may pretend to drop dead. It lies stiffly on the ground with its tongue hanging out. Its eyes glaze over. A foul-smelling greenish liquid oozes from its rear end. Or, instead of playing dead, it might drool, vomit or poo and pee on itself. After all that, most predators give up.

Revolting meals

Common Virginia opossums live in most parts of North America. They are opportunistic feeders. This means they will eat whatever they can find.

Some of their food is really revolting. They will eat cockroaches, slugs, rats and even runover animals! They also eat plants, nuts and berries.

Opossums usually come out at night. During the day they curl up in hollow logs, or even in garages and attics.

Growing up in a pouch

Opossums are a type of **mammal** known as a **marsupial.** Marsupials give birth to babies that are not fully developed.

Newborn opossums are tiny, hairless and helpless. Twenty of them would fit in a teaspoon. They need to grow some more, so they crawl into a pouch on their mother's tummy. Inside the pouch, the babies drink their mother's milk and keep growing.

The babies stay in the pouch for about two months, then they come out. But they still need their mother's help. For the next few weeks they may ride around on her back. She teaches them how to avoid **predators** and how to find food. By the time the babies are five months old, they are ready to go off on their own.

The common Virginia opossum can wrap its tail around a tree branch and hang upside down.

Did you know?

The common opossum is the only marsupial that is native to North America.

Which bald-headed bird eats dead material?

In a bird beauty contest, the lappet-faced vulture would probably come last. Its head and neck are bald. And it has a big, ugly hooked beak. But what it does with its head is even uglier. It plunges its head deep into the bodies of dead animals and eats the rotting flesh, or **carrion**!

A messy eater

Being ugly works out well for the lappet-faced vulture. Carrion is swarming with **bacteria**. If the vulture had a feathered head, bits of rotting meat and bacteria would get stuck in the feathers. The bald head and neck are an **adaptation**. Being bald makes it easier for the vulture to clean itself after a meal.

The lappet-faced vulture is named for the flaps of skin, or lappets, on the sides of its head.

King of the carrion

The lappet-faced vulture lives in the deserts and grasslands of Africa. It is one of the largest vultures in Africa. Its wingspan is 3 metres. That's wider than most sofas.

Like all vultures, the lappet-faced vulture is a **scavenger.** Scavengers do not usually kill their own **prey.** When a lion or tiger kills an animal, it eats what it wants and then leaves. Vultures of several **species** then take over.

Other species let lappet-faced vultures eat first. Lappet-faced vultures are the only species that have beaks that can rip through the tough skin of large animals. Sometimes other vultures wait near **carrion** until a lappet-faced vulture turns up to help them out.

This lappet-faced vulture is eating a dead gazelle.

Did you know?

Lappet-faced vultures line their nests with fur plucked from the dead animals they eat.

Which snake tries to disgust its enemies?

The eastern hognose snake puts on a disgusting show when a **predator** threatens it. First, it flattens its head until it is two or three times wider than normal. It hisses, lunges and poos. Next, it thrashes around and throws up.

Finally, the snake flops over on its back with its tongue sticking out. It lies there, looking dead, until the predator leaves.

Usually the predator does not stick around. The eastern hognose snake looks and smells far too disgusting.

The eastern hognose snake has a snout that looks something like a pig's (hog's) nose. The snake uses this snout to help dig itself an underground burrow.

Did you know?

If a baby eastern hognose snake gets scared while it is hatching, it starts acting out its own death even before it has crawled all the way out of its egg.

A day in the life of a hognose

The eastern hognose snake is a **reptile** that lives east of the Rocky Mountains in North America. It lives in forests, prairies and grasslands. When not acting out a grand death scene, the eastern hognose snake **basks** in the sun or slithers around looking for food.

If you place a 'dead' eastern hognose snake right side up, it will immediately flip itself back over and play dead again.

The eastern hognose snake eats small reptiles, **mammals** and insects. But mainly it eats toads. The snake has special **adaptations** for toad eating. Toads sometimes puff themselves up with air to make themselves larger and harder to eat. The eastern hognose snake can deal with this. It has a very wide mouth and stretchy jaws. This helps it get its mouth around a toad. It also has special fangs to prick a hole in the toad. This lets the air out and makes the toad easier to swallow.

Which amphibians look like creepy blind worms?

Worms look creepy, but caecilians look even creepier! For one thing, they are usually a lot bigger than the average earthworm. The largest **species** of caecilian is 1.5 metres long. Also, caecilians look as if they have no eyes. Their eyes are hidden under their skin.

Legless wonders

Caecilians are a type of legless **amphibian** that lives in Africa, Asia and Central and South America. Most live underground. A few species live in ponds or streams. They have poor eyesight. But they have a special organ that gives them a very good sense of smell. They use this to sniff out the earthworms, insects and **larvae** that they eat.

Caecilians use their hard, pointed heads for digging.

From squishy egg to slimy worm

Most caecilians give birth to live babies. But some **species** lay eggs. The soft eggs come out of the female's body attached to each other in a long, sticky string. The female then bundles the eggs into a ball and curls her body around it. She does this to guard the eggs from **predators**. She also does this so she can check for eggs that have been attacked by **fungi** and killed. If she finds a dead egg, she eats it. But besides dead eggs, she eats nothing until her eggs hatch.

It can take ten to eleven weeks for the eggs to hatch. In some species, the young that hatch are miniature adult caecilians. In other species, however, the young are **larvae**. As time passes, they go through a change, or **metamorphosis**. They lose the **gill** slits that help them breathe in water and the shape of their head changes.

A female caecilian of the species Ichthyophis kohtaoensis *lays about 30 eggs.*

Which fish is a slimebucket?

The hagfish is nicknamed the 'slime eel'. This slippery fish has about 200 slime glands on its body. In a few minutes it can make enough thick, slimy **mucus** to fill a bucket!

Slippery characters

The hagfish's sliminess is an **adaptation** for stopping its enemies. When threatened, the hagfish covers itself in a thick coat of mucus. Predators that attack end up with a mouth so full of slime that they choke.

Sometimes the hagfish gets too slimy for its own liking. It then ties itself in a knot. It slips the knot down its body, which pushes the slime off.

A slimy hagfish may grow to be 80 centimetres long.

Did you know?

A hagfish has five hearts. One heart carries blood to the head. Another takes blood to the gills, and yet another pumps blood to the hagfish's organs. The two other hearts move blood from the tail.

It's an ugly body, but it works

The hagfish lives in the colder parts of the sea. It usually stays on the bottom with most of its body buried in mud.

Unlike most fish, the hagfish has no jaw, no stomach and no bones. Its eyes are pretty useless because they are under a layer of skin. But the hagfish manages without all these things.

Hagfish also eat marine worms and other invertebrates.

The hagfish's skeleton is made from a flexible (bends easily) material called cartilage, which helps it wiggle its way around. Its bad eyesight is not a problem either. It has a good sense of smell and a set of six feelers around its mouth that help it find **prey**. And as for a jaw, who needs it? The hagfish's tongue has a set of sharp, pointed teeth that can do plenty of damage.

*Getting all knotted up can help a hagfish slip out of a **predator's** grasp.*

Terrible table manners

The hagfish has disgusting eating habits. It eats dead fish. Sometimes it does not even wait for its prey to die. It uses its toothed tongue to drill itself into the fish's body. Then it eats the fish's insides. When the hagfish has finished, all that is left of its victim are its skin and bones.

The hagfish's bloodsucking cousin

Lampreys are **parasites** that live in oceans and in freshwater. A lamprey's mouth looks like a suction cup with teeth. When it is hungry, it attaches this sucker mouth to a fish. It then sucks the blood and the life right out of its victim. Sea lampreys that have made their way into the Great Lakes in the USA have killed large numbers of **native** fish. People are working to get rid of them there.

Which mollusc looks like a rotten banana?

Imagine you are walking in the woods on the west coast of the USA. You look down and see what looks like a skinny banana with blotchy, black peel. The thing is inching its way across the forest floor, leaving behind a sticky trail of slime. Yuck!

A banana slug's eyes are at the end of its feelers.

Did you know?

Slugs can stretch up to 20 times their normal length, to squeeze through narrow openings to reach food.

The banana slug is a **mollusc** that lives in forests near the Pacific coast of North America. They are quite large. The average banana slug is 15 to 20 centimetres long. That's about the length of a small banana. Some are nearly 25 centimetres long.

The banana slug is a **decomposer**. It eats mucky things like dead leaves and **fungi**. It also eats the poo of other forest animals. When it eats these foods, it breaks them down and returns **nutrients** to the forest soil. The nutrients help forest plants grow strong and healthy.

A slimy way of life

Slime is very important to the banana slug. The slug breathes through a small lung and through its skin. The skin is kept moist with slimy **mucus**. Mucus also helps the banana slug move. Slippery mucus from the slug's body creates a little trail that helps the slug glide over rough areas.

Slime is also the banana slug's secret weapon. If a duck or a goose tries to eat the slug, it rolls itself into a ball and starts oozing slime. Most birds then spit out the slug to avoid choking.

Which insect loves poo?

Dung is another word for **faeces**, which is another word for poo! And the dung beetle really lives up to its name. The dung beetle collects poo, makes poo balls, digs in poo, raises babies in poo, and steals poo. Last, but not least, it eats poo.

A world of dung

Dung beetles are insects that live wherever there is good supply of poo, which is everywhere except Antarctica. Many **species** of dung beetle live in the grasslands of Africa. This is where a lot of large **mammals** live. Nothing makes a dung beetle happier than a huge pile of rhino, hippo or elephant poo.

An army of 16,000 dung beetles can make a 2.2-kilogram elephant poo disappear in two hours or less.

Did you know?

One kind of dung beetle lives near a wallaby's bottom. (Wallabies are related to kangaroos.) This way it always has fresh poo to lay eggs in. The larvae eat the poo.

What do they do with it all?

Different types of dung beetles do different things with the dung. Tiny dung beetles known as dwellers live inside mounds of dung. 'Tunnellers' dig under the pile and store the dung in tunnels for safekeeping. 'Rollers' use their mouths and legs to build a dung ball. Then they roll the ball away from other beetles that might steal it.

A life of poo

Poo is a part of all stages of a dung beetle's life. For example, 'roller' dung beetles often meet a **mate** on a dung heap. Once a male and female have paired off, they dig an underground nest and roll dung balls into it. The female lays one egg on each ball. When the larvae hatch, they eat their way out of the dung. When they crawl out of the ground as adults, they make their way to the nearest fresh dung for more feasting.

Dung beetles can build dung balls as large as apples.

21

A nasty job but someone's got to do it

We should be thankful for dung beetles. Dung beetles are **decomposers.** They eat and bury poo, which helps put **nutrients** back into the soil.

Many male dung beetles have horns on their heads which they use when fighting over a piece of dung.

In Australia, dung beetles are being put to work. In the 1960s, Australia's **native** dung beetles could no longer keep up with all the dung piling up in cow and sheep fields. Flies that **breed** on dung had become a huge pest and health problem.

The Australian government brought in other **species** of dung beetle, which soon brought the dung and fly problem under control.

Did you know?

In five hours, Australia's cattle herds produce about three cowpats for every person living in Australia! That's 12 million cowpats!

Which insect sucks the blood of sleepers?

Bedbugs are insect vampires. They suck blood. Any **warm-blooded** animal, including birds, bats, cats and humans may become their victim.

They only come out at night

Bedbugs live in most parts of the world. During the day they hide. If it is human blood they are after, they may hide in the cracks of walls, under peeling wallpaper, or in mattresses. They also hide in bat caves, birds' nests and henhouses.

At night bedbugs leave their hiding places and find a sleeping victim. Their needle-like mouthparts prick the sleeper's skin.

Bedbugs are **parasites**. Blood of other animals is the only thing they eat. Blood is rich in **nutrients**.

Bedbugs are about 6 millimetres long, or about the size of a pea.

The masked bedbug hunter
What's worse than sucking the blood of sleepers? How about drinking that blood after a bedbug has sucked it up? The masked bedbug hunter does this. It stabs a bedbug with its mouthparts and sucks the secondhand blood out of it.

A bedbug's meal usually lasts three to five minutes.

Eating in bed

The bedbugs squirt a fluid into the bite to make the blood flow more easily. Then they suck up the blood. When a bedbug has finished, its body is swollen red with blood. It may not need another meal for a year!

If a bedbug's victim is a human, that person will wake up with a very itchy bite. The fluid that the bedbug spurted into the bite causes the itching.

It is not easy to prove that a person was bitten by bedbugs. But bedbugs do leave a few clues. There may be a stink in the air. Bedbugs have glands that give off an oily smell. Also, the sheets may have small brownish stains on them. These are bedbug poo.

Which flowers make a big stink?

The dead-horse arum flower stinks so much that it attracts flies. The titan arum may be even worse. It smells so horrible that people have passed out after getting a whiff of it.

The titan arum grows on the Indonesian island of Sumatra. The dead-horse arum grows on islands in the Mediterranean Sea.

Smelly and ugly

These plants smell like rotting meat or fish. They are not very pretty. The bottom of their bloom, called a spathe, looks like a raggedy skirt. A thick, cigar-shaped growth, called a spadix, rises out of the spathe. Clusters of tiny flowers are found at the bottom of the spadix.

The titan arum only blooms for a few days.

25

What's all the stink about?

Scientists have tested the smell of a rotting animal and the smell of a dead-horse arum. They found that the smells are almost the same! There is a very good reason why these flowers smell so terrible. The odour attracts flies that **breed** on **carrion**. When the flies visit the flowers, they **pollinate** them.

The dead-horse arum often grows near seagull colonies. Flies that feed on rotting fish left behind by gulls find the smell of the dead-horse arum even more inviting.

When a fly finds a dead-horse arum, it dives deep inside to get to the source of the horrid stink. Once inside, the fly discovers it cannot get out. Stiff hairs block the way.

After a few days, the flowers above the hairs shed pollen on the fly. Once this happens, the hairs shrivel and the fly can leave. When the fly moves into the next arum, the pollen on its body will pollinate that plant.

Letting off some foul steam

The titan arum can be smelled far and wide. When it is ready to be pollinated, the spadix heats up. The tip can reach temperatures close to human body temperature, which is 37 °C.

The heat helps the stench travel further. This increases the titan arum's chances of attracting flies and beetles to pollinate it. Once an insect gets inside a titum arum, it finds itself trapped in the same way insects were trapped by the dead-horse arum. The insect cannot escape until it has had some pollen sprinkled on it.

The rhinoceros hornbill helps spread the seeds of the titan arum in its droppings.

Did you know?

Not all arums stink. There is a species that smells like bananas and one that smells like chocolate.

☑ The common housefly has to throw up saliva on its food before it can eat it. Chemicals in the saliva help break down the food into a liquid. The housefly can then suck up the liquid meal through its straw-like mouthparts.

☑ Several **species** of spider look like bird droppings. This helps them attract certain insects that eat bird droppings because of the salts in them. The spiders then eat the insects they attract. Looking like bird poo also turns off predators that might otherwise eat the spider.

☑ The western hook-nosed snake tries to scare off **predators** by farting. The snake may put enough energy into the fart to lift itself off the ground.

☑ The smell of the durian fruit has been compared to sweaty socks, rotting rubbish and overripe cheese. Yet many people say it tastes wonderful. But if it is not eaten right away, it rots quickly. In some Southeast Asian countries where, it grows, it is illegal to eat a durian in public buildings.

This is the caterpillar of the orchard swallow butterfly. It looks like bird poo. This is a great defence. Predators do not want to eat bird poo.

☑ Leeches are a type of worm that can suck blood. The giant Amazon leech can reach 50 centimetres, or about the length of your arm.

Young fulmar birds spew a stream of awful-smelling yellow stomach oil when a predator gets close. Chicks that are just a few days old can hit targets nearly 30 centimetres away. As they get older, they can hit a predator as far away as 1.5 metres.

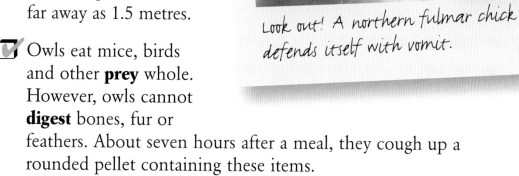

Look out! A northern fulmar chick defends itself with vomit.

Owls eat mice, birds and other **prey** whole. However, owls cannot **digest** bones, fur or feathers. About seven hours after a meal, they cough up a rounded pellet containing these items.

A shrike, also known as a butcherbird, sometimes skewers its prey on thorns. It then takes the insect, mouse or bird apart piece by piece and eats it.

Black vultures and turkey vultures poo and pee on their legs. It is thought that this might cool them off in hot weather.

Glossary

adaptation   special feature that helps a plant or animal survive

amphibian   animal that lives part of its life in water and part of its life on land

bacteria   very tiny lifeforms that can only be seen with a microscope. Some bacteria cause diseases.

bask   warm up in the sun

breed   male and female come together so they will have babies

carrion   dead, rotting animal flesh

decomposer   animal that breaks down rotting matter

digest   break down food so it can be absorbed

faeces   solid animal waste

fungus   (more than one are fungi) organism such as mold, mildew and mushrooms

gill   opening in a fish or amphibian's body that lets it breathe underwater

larva   (more than one are called larvae) early wormlike stage in the life of some animals

mammal   animal that is warm-blooded, has hair or fur, a backbone and drinks milk made by its mother

marsupial   mammal whose young are not fully developed at birth

mate   partner with whom an animal makes babies

metamorphosis   change in an animal's body of size, shape and function

mollusc   soft-bodied animal that has no bones

mucus   slimy substance produced by an animal's body

native   plant or animal that has always lived in a particular area

nutrient   food substance that a plant or animal needs to survive

parasite   animal or plant that gets its food by living on or in another animal or plant

pollinate   carry a dusty substance (pollen) made by flowers from one part of a flower to another or from one plant to another plant

predator   animal that hunts, kills and eats another type of animal

prey   animal that is hunted by other animals for food

reptile   cold-blooded animal with a backbone and scaly skin that breathes through lungs and lays eggs

scavenger animal that eats dead prey that has been killed by another animal

species group of animals that have the same features and can have babies with each other

urine liquid animal waste

warm-blooded able to keep the body temperature always the same

More books to read

Amazing Nature: Pesky Parasites, John Woodward
(Heinemann Library, 2004)

From Egg to Adult: The Life Cycle of Insects, Mike Unwin
(Heinemann Library, 2003)

Go Facts: Reptiles, Paul McEvoy
(A & C Black, 2003)

Hidden Life: What's Living in Your Bedroom?, Andrew Solway
(Heinemann Library, 2004)

Life in a Cave, Clare Oliver
(Evans, 2003)

The Secret World of Snakes, Theresa Greenaway
(Raintree, 2002)

The Variety of Life: Molluscs, Joy Richardson
(Franklin Watts, 2003)

Index